D1505747

580*

Tutankhamen's Treasures
John Ford

CHARTWELL BOOKS INC.

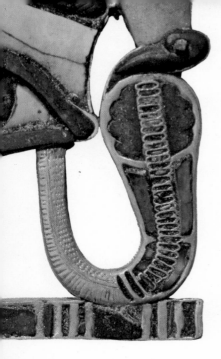

Contents

Designed and produced by
Albany Books
36 Park Street London W1Y 4DE

First published 1978

Published by Chartwell Books Inc.
A Division of Book Sales Inc.
110 Enterprise Avenue
Secaucus, New Jersey 07094

Text copyright © Albany Books 1978
Illustrations (except endpapers) ©
Copyright George Rainbird Ltd 1963

Printed in Hong Kong

All rights reserved. No part of this
publication may be reproduced, stored
in a retrieval system or transmitted in
any form or by any means, electronic,
mechanical, photocopying, recording or
otherwise, without the prior permission
of the copyright owner.

*Endpapers: The tomb of Tutankhamen
showing the outermost mummiform coffin lying
in the great quartzite sarcophagus. The wall
paintings show rituals of death (MacQuitty
International Collection).*

1 The Discovery

Above: A pendant representing Nekhabet, the vulture goddess of Southern Egypt.

On 4 November 1922, in the pale, golden light of an autumn morning, a gang of Egyptian workmen were carefully digging in the hills opposite Thebes. As they prised away the foundations of an ancient hut, their voices merged with the rhythmic sound of picks striking against stone. Suddenly, unexpectedly, there was silence; and that in itself was enough to alert their employer, an archaeologist named Howard Carter, to the importance of the occasion.

What they had uncovered seemed modest enough – a step cut into the rock below – yet it aroused a fever of anticipation in everyone present. By the next afternoon fifteen more steps

had been exposed, leading sharply down to a doorway, blocked with stone. There, impressed in the plaster facing, was a series of priestly seals, including two of great significance. Near the top was the image of a jackal with nine captives, the mark of a royal tomb; and lower down the sign for Nebkheprure: the coronation name of the pharaoh Tutankhamen.

For Carter, that sight was the reward for ten years' labour and he was sorely tempted to tear the wall down there and then. Yet with supreme self-control, he ordered his men to cover the steps once more and, leaving the site well guarded, began the

preparations for a ceremonial opening. The first priority was to telegraph his patron, Lord Carnavon, who received the momentous news at Highclere Castle, his ancestral home in southern England. The message read: 'At last you have made a wonderful discovery in Valley; a magnificent tomb with seals intact; re-covered same for your arrival. Congratulations. Carter.'

The partnership between these two men was a classic product of the British Empire, to which Egypt had effectively belonged since 1882. They came from opposite ends of the social ladder. Carnavon was an extremely wealthy and cultured aristocrat, whose main interests as a young man had been sport and travel. He had gone to Egypt in 1902 to recuperate from a serious automobile accident, and was encouraged to take up archaeology by the Consul-General, Lord Cromer. In contrast, Carter had begun life as a draughtsman and had worked his way up from a minor post in the Egyptian Department of Antiquities. By the time he was introduced to Carnavon in 1907, he had reached the position of Chief Inspector of the Theban Necropolis.

Their mutual interests were readily apparent. Carter had little money of his own, and excavation was a long and expensive business, requiring large teams of skilled workmen. Systematic digging of a major site could take several years, for excavation was possible only during the cooler months of winter. Carnavon, on the other hand, could not proceed without expert help, and since he was eager to dig at Thebes, the richest and most important site in Egypt, Carter was the ideal man for the job. From 1908 to 1912, therefore, the two men explored the royal burial grounds in the Valley of Kings with encour-

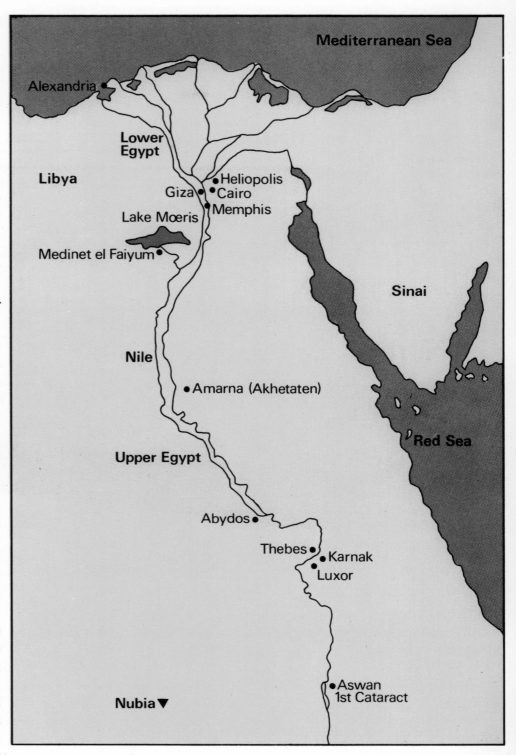

aging, if not spectacular, results.

Like most archaeologists, Carter was searching principally for knowledge, for those scraps of information that would enable him to build up our picture of the past, rather than for treasure. In any case, the notion that anyone might find a pharaoh's grave intact was no more than an inspiring daydream, hardly to be

Above: Sketch map of Egypt.

Left: A double container used for holy oils or perfumes.

9

Above: A chest made of stuccoed wood, painted with scenes of Tutankhamen in his chariot.

taken seriously. For centuries, the tombs had been pillaged repeatedly by the local villagers, who showed great ingenuity in discovering their locations and regarded them as a private resource to be drawn on in times of need.

Furthermore, nearly all the kings known to have been buried at Thebes had been accounted for by the time Carter and Carnavon began their search. Theodore Davis, an American who unearthed sixteen tombs in a period of seven years from 1903 to 1908, found most of them virtually empty and wrote in the preface of his book: 'I fear that the Valley of the Kings is now exhausted.'

With the outbreak of World War

I, Carnavon left Egypt, but Carter continued to search periodically and was even rewarded by the discovery of two more graves. Then, from 1919 to 1921, he carefully prospected a further sector of the valley. The results were still fairly meagre, but in a small pit at the western end he found some jar sealings bearing the name of Tutankhamen – a relatively unknown pharaoh whose tomb had never been found. By the end of that season Carter's map showed only one small area of the valley still to be dug.

Then, in the summer of 1922, Carnavon decided to abandon the excavation. Summoning Carter to Highclere, he explained that the expense could no longer be justified;

Right: The death mask of the pharaoh, made of solid gold, shows him wearing the false beard of the Gods, but is otherwise a close likeness.

Left: *A head of the sacred cow Hathor, goddess of the heavens.*

Below: *The lid of an alabaster jar, showing a fledgling in a nest of eggs.*

and he was scarcely convinced by Carter's suggestion that another season might yet prove worthwhile. Nonetheless, he reluctantly agreed to finance one last effort.

In the event, it took just four days to find the missing tomb. Carnavon hurried out to Egypt as soon as he received the news, arriving in Thebes on 23 November. The next day, with the steps cleared once more, the two men led a small party of observers to the entrance of the tomb. Even at that moment of intense excitement, Carter's patience was unshakeable. He examined the doorway for the second time with meticulous care, and the tension increased with the disturbing realization that the tomb had after all been entered long before. A hole just large enough for a man to crawl through had been made, then re-filled. Yet the position of the seals showed that the robbery had been in ancient times, and that priests had repaired the damage.

As the others waited anxiously behind him, Carter made a small hole in the corner of the door. For the first time in 3000 years, a ray of light pierced the gloom. Holding a candle into the space beyond, he stared into the darkness. Gradually

a sense of anti-climax dawned upon him: he was looking along a passageway strewn with rubble but otherwise empty. It would be four more days before the little group could gather again to repeat their vigil at a second door.

By then the excitement was even greater, as Carter peered once more into the dark. 'At first I could see nothing, the hot air from the chamber causing the candle to flicker. But presently, as my eyes grew accustomed to the light, details of the room emerged slowly from the mist, strange animals, statues, and gold – everywhere the glint of gold. For a moment – an eternity it must have seemed to the others standing by, I was struck

dumb.' Even from that first glance it was apparent that the thieves could only have taken the smallest items.

For a few short hours Carter, Carnavon and their close associates experienced an unrepeatable sense of elation. For the first time ever, the tomb of an Egyptian pharaoh had been discovered intact – and they alone had seen it. Within days, however, they had become the centre of world attention, overwhelmed by reporters, tourists and visitors of all kinds. Quarrels were not long in breaking out. Carter, short-tempered by nature, was incensed by the constant interruptions. It would take six years in all to remove the treasures and pre-

Above: A magnificent chest of wood and ivory, with sixteen separate compartments.

Right: The goddess Serket guards a small shrine. On her head is a scorpion, symbolizing her magic powers.

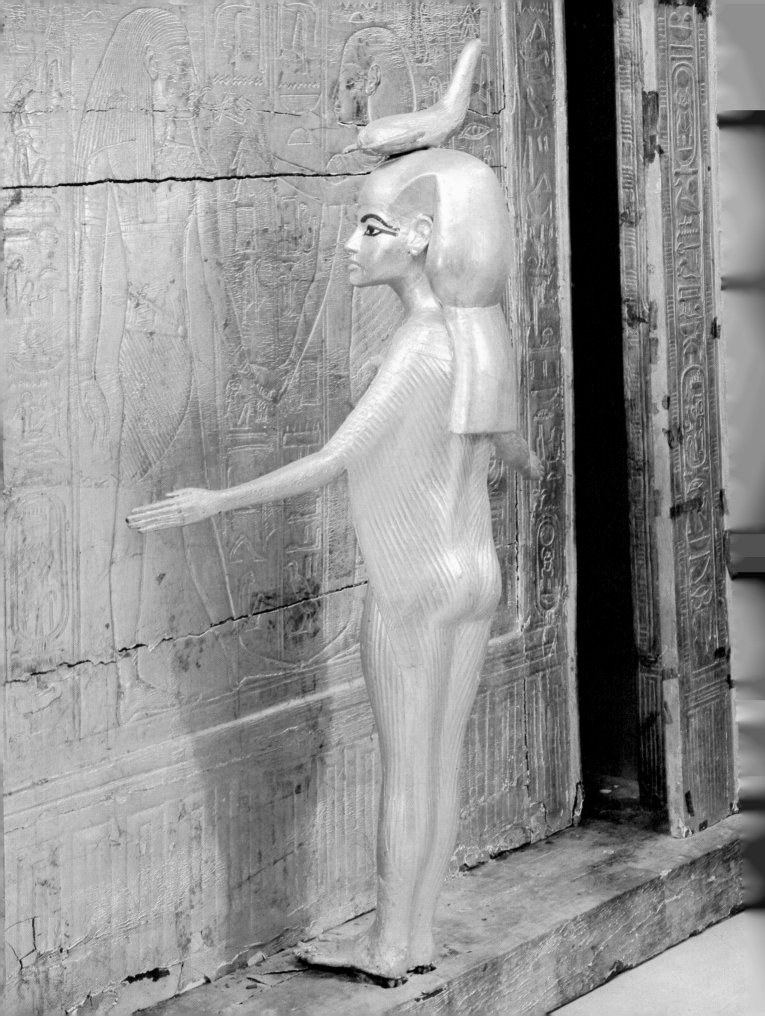

serve them for posterity; not surprisingly, he was weighed down by the responsibility. At one point, Carter and the entire archaeological team resigned in protest at the conditions they were forced to endure. For a full nine months Carter suffered agonies, as less able men continued the work before they were brought back.

Relations between Carter and his patron were also broken off. Carnavon, who had spent vast sums pursuing the excavation, believed he was entitled to a proportion of the find. This suggestion roused Carter to a fury, and in February 1923 he ordered his former patron to leave his house.

Not long afterwards there was a drama of a different kind, when Lord Carnavon died of pneumonia in a Cairo hospital; inexplicably the lights of the city went out at that precise moment and, far away at Highclere, the nobleman's dog

howled inconsolably and died. For the popular press it was obvious that Carnavon had incurred the pharaoh's curse and, when two other members of the archaeological team died within a few years, the story grew more lurid still. Carter, however, lived until 1939, and several others survived into the 1960s.

By the time the tomb had finally been emptied, Carter and his colleagues had carefully examined, restored and catalogued more than 2000 items, whose permanent home is now the Cairo Museum. They range from food and drink, in the form of mummified ducks, chunks of beef and fine vintage wines; to weapons, chariots and ritual furniture such as beds, thrones and couches; to clothing and jewellery; and even to touching mementoes of the pharaoh's youth – a small box containing string, some pebbles and a few simple toys. Carter was to estimate that sixty per cent of the gems

Top right: An alabaster vase inlaid with glass paste in the form of lotus petals.

Right: An alabaster wishing-cup, whose inscription reads: 'Mayest thou spend millions of years, O thou who lovest Thebes, seated with thy face turned to the north wind and thine eyes contemplating felicity.'

Left: A life-like model of the young king, in painted and stuccoed wood.

had been taken by the thieves, but the treasure that remained was enough to demonstrate the fabulous wealth of the ancient Egyptians.

Yet the events of the king's life remained vague and uncertain. Although he was mentioned in the 'king-lists' kept by Egyptian priests, few statues of him remained outside the tomb and his role in history was far from clear. Only by a slow process of deduction has it been possible to piece together the main elements of his reign. Over the last fifty years the archaeological detectives have gradually revealed the extraordinary story of a young king sentenced to obscurity by his successors, but resurrected after 3000 years by the patient endeavours of a most determined man – Howard Carter.

Top: A heavy ear-ring, probably worn by Tutankhamen as a boy: his ears would have been pierced in childhood.

Right: A pendant representing the winged scarab, symbol of immortality, attended by the goddesses Isis and Nephthys.

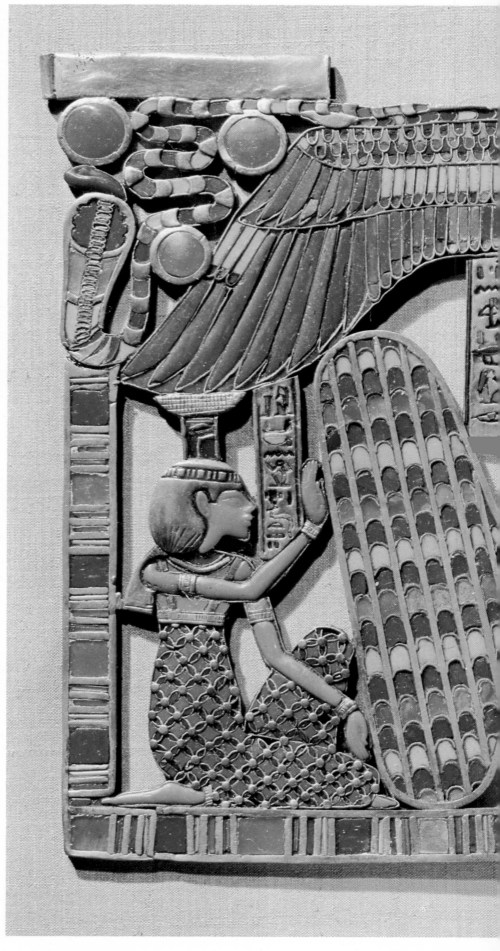

2 Land of the Pharaohs

Above: A pendant representing the 'eye of Horus' flanked by the vulture of the Southern Kingdom and the serpent of the North.

Even today, the sun and the river Nile are the pillars of life in Egypt. All year round, the weather is warm and dry, parching the vast deserts that roll across North Africa; but along the narrow, winding strip formed by the Nile, the soil is abundantly fertile. Each spring, when the rain clouds of the Indian Ocean drench the highlands of East Africa, the Nile and its tributaries rush a vast burden of rich, black silt down through the rocky gorges of Sudan to spread it at the feet of the

Egyptians. As the sun evaporates the floods, planting is easy and for the labour of a few weeks an entire year's crops can be grown.

Occasionally, however, conditions are extreme and there is too much or too little water. Today, the giant dam at Aswan regulates the flow, but in ancient times floods might overwhelm whole villages, or scarcity bring a year of famine. Perhaps it was the pressure of necessity that led, 5000 years ago, to the unification of Egypt under a single king

Left: The head of a funerary couch in the form of Tueris, the Hippopotamus goddess.

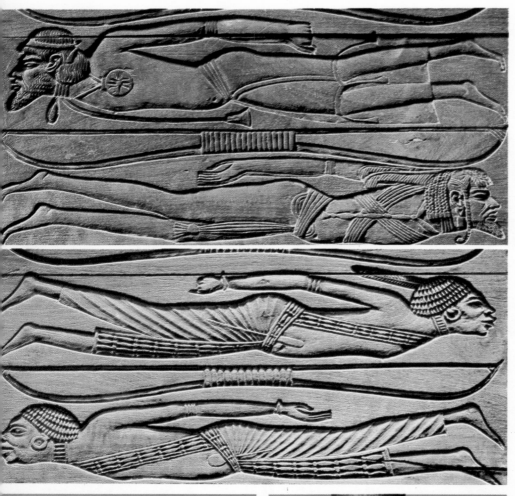

or pharaoh. For centuries, the villages of the Delta area had been grouped together as the Kingdom of Lower Egypt; those to the south as Upper Egypt. Around 3000 BC, a warrior traditionally known as Menes led the armies of the South to victory over the North and established a new capital at Memphis, where the kingdoms joined.

Within a very short time, the pharaohs had imposed such an effective centralized administration that the peasants of the Nile villages could be 'called up' each year during the three months of inactivity while the floods covered the fields, to labour on dams, irrigation canals, reservoirs and other public works. Gradually the river was harnessed to the country's needs – and at the same time, the power and wealth of the pharaohs grew to staggering proportions. Their authority was not maintained solely by force, however. Egypt at this time had no permanent army, although local nobles were expected to provide soldiers when required. The long-term stability of the social order depended rather on the genuine belief that the pharaohs were gods.

Religion in Egyptian life was all pervasive and, as in India today, literally hundreds of different deities were worshipped. All were associated with natural phenomena – for example, animals such as the crocodile, the bull and the lion, and cosmic forces such as the wind, the storm and, most important of all, the

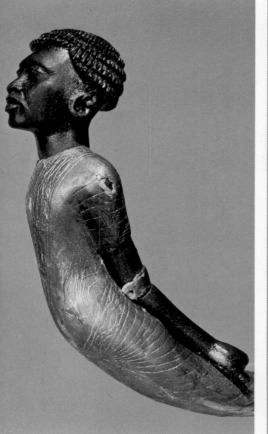

Top left: Carvings on Tutankhamen's ceremonial footstool show Egypt's traditional enemies, the Asians and the Africans, prostrate and defeated.

Left: Details of ceremonial canes show the two traditional enemies of Egypt.

Right: The goddess Isis, wife of Osiris and mother of Horus.

sun. There was no strict hierarchy of gods, but some became more prominent than others through their association with particular towns or areas that became important in themselves. It was in this way that the sun god Re, with his main shrines at Heliopolis, near Memphis, was closely identified with the royal capital and that the pharaohs came to be regarded as his sons.

For about 1000 years, during the period now known as the Old Kingdom, the pharaohs maintained their absolute authority. This was the time when the massive stone pyramids were built, as tombs for the divine kings. Temples to the sun god were richly endowed, and the influence of the priesthood grew stead-

ily. Around 2000 BC, however, the local nobility came to challenge the central powers, and when the monarchy emerged dominant once more, during the era of the Middle Kingdom, the capital was moved south to Thebes. The most important deity here was Amun, but to take advantage of the prestige still attaching to Memphis, he was declared to be another aspect of Re, and henceforth known as Amun-Re.

An equally fascinating development at this time was the rise of the Osiris cult, centred on Abydos, to the north-east of Thebes. A cluster of related beliefs explained the origin of the world and the sequence of life and death; from this time on, it was central to Egyptian burial

Above: Tutankhamen in his chariot, guided and protected by the winged serpent and the vulture.

Right: Details from Tutankhamen's chariot show (top) the king as a sphinx, crushing his enemies, and (bottom) the victims taken captive.

customs. According to these myths, only the ocean had existed at first. Then a flower appeared, from which was born the sun god, who in turn created the gods of the earth (Geb), the sky (Nut) and the atmosphere. Geb and Nut had four children: Osiris, Isis, Nephthys and Seth.

When Osiris married Isis and succeeded Geb as ruler of the earth, Seth became jealous. Killing his brother, he cut the body into pieces which he buried in various parts of Egypt. Abydos was where the head was buried. When Isis discovered what had happened, she carefully collected all the pieces and re-assembled her husband's body with the help of the jackal god Anubis. Osiris now became god of the dead,

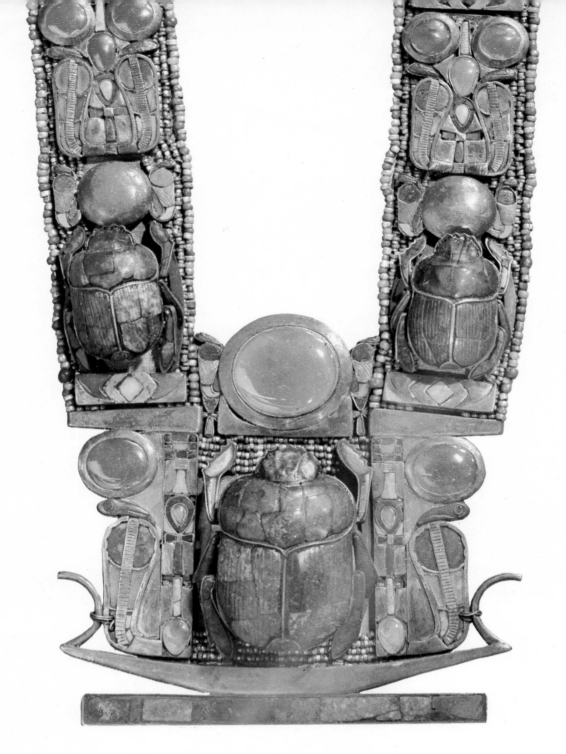

and Isis gave birth to his son, Horus, who revenged his father by killing Seth.

As the Middle Kingdom priests had amalgamated Amun with Re as the sun god, and hence the father of Osiris, these myths eventually formed the solid core of Egyptian religion. A tomb at Abydos was declared to be that of Osiris himself and a carving of the god was placed over the shrine, which became a

centre of pilgrimage. In fact, the occupant of the tomb was one of the first pharaohs – a clear indication that the rulers were now being deliberately identified with the Osiris cult. Put in the simplest terms, the pharaoh while living was regarded as a manifestation of Horus; when dead he became an aspect of Osiris. The rituals that accompanied major events in the king's reign, from coronation to burial, were all de-

Above: A pendant representing a boat with a scarab holding the solar globe, and protected by two serpents.

Top right: An alabaster lamp in the form of three lotus flowers.

Bottom right: An elaborate ring bezel shows Tutankhamen between two dog-headed monkeys, worshipping Horus. Two sacred birds, a vulture and a falcon, stretch out their wings around them.

26

signed to ensure the smooth transition from one phase of the divine existence to the next.

During the Middle Kingdom, the pharaohs extended Egyptian power beyond the traditional boundaries – the deserts to the east and west, the Nile cataracts to the south and the Sinai peninsula to the north-east. Military expeditions were successfully made into Syria and Nubia (on the borders of modern Sudan). By 1600 BC, however, it was Egypt's turn to be occupied; a gradual infiltration by the technically more advanced Hyksos people from the north resulted in 150 years of foreign rule. When Pharaoh Ahmose finally drove the Hyksos back into Palestine after generations of resistance, he opened an era of massive imperial expansion that would be pursued by all his successors until Amenophis III, the father of Tutankhamen.

In this early part of what is now known as the New Kingdom, Egypt controlled a vast area stretching from Nubia to the Euphrates river, in northern Syria. Vassal states, sometimes subject to military occupation, paid annual tribute to the pharaohs in the form of precious metals, jewels, slaves, animals and luxury goods of all kinds. With Amun's priesthood once again exerting political influence, much of the tribute was diverted into the temples, most notably those at Karnak and Luxor, close to Thebes.

When it became clear that Amenophis III had no intention of following his ancestors in the path of conquest, the latent conflict between priesthood and pharaoh came slowly to a head. One by one, the vassals furthest away began tentatively to withhold tribute. The priesthood demanded immediate action; Amenophis demurred. To counteract the priests of Amun, he encouraged those of Re, at Heliopolis, and towards the end of his reign

assisted his oldest son and co-regent, Amenophis IV, in a full-blooded revolt against the established religion.

Amenophis IV announced his heresy by building a new palace complex some 320 kilometres down the Nile at Amarna. There he abandoned both Amun and the Osiris cult, devoting himself exclusively to Aten – the sun god in his material aspect as the solar globe. He even changed his own name to Akhenaten and named his new city Akhetaten in honour of the single deity. Nor did the revolution stop there: a new style in art emerged, demystifying the traditions of the past. The pharaoh was shown not as a god, but as he really was – somewhat round-shouldered and with large hips. The city's necropolis, instead of being on the west side according to Osirian practice, was built on the east.

When Akhenaten succeeded his father he took more violent measures against the priesthood. Agents were sent throughout the kingdom to tear down statues of other gods, particularly those of Amun. The

Left: A tiny statuette of Amenophis III, made of solid gold.

Below: The king's golden dagger and its sheath, decorated with hunting scenes.

great temples at Karnak and Luxor fell into disrepair. Even then, the authority of the pharaoh was not seriously threatened. His main adviser, Ay, was Commander of the King's Horse and Lieutenant-General of the Chariots; the army was prepared to play a passive role, waiting to see how events continued. The news from the vassal states, however, was not promising. Some north Syrian provinces were already independent, others were withholding tribute. Unless this trend could be reversed, other generals – most notably Horemheb, in charge of the Asian armies – might turn against the throne.

Towards the end of his life, it seems that Akhenaten was seeking a compromise with the Amun priesthood. He took as co-regent his brother Smenkhkare, who moved back to Thebes, thereby restoring prestige to the city. Time now was on the side of the priests, for not only was Smenkhkare there, but also a child about eight years old. The youngest son of Amenophis III and an obvious candidate for the throne, the boy had been brought up in the heretic faith, but was innocent enough to be controlled by older men. Thus, when both Akhenaten and Smenkhkare died in the same year, probably 1361 BC, a youth called Tutankh*aten* became pharaoh of Egypt. It would not be long before he changed his name.

Above: An elaborate pendant representing a winged scarab supporting the boat of the sun god, which contains the 'eye of Horus' Above it, on the disc of the darkened sun, the gods Thoth and Horus guide Tutankhamen towards eternal life.

29

3 Tutankhamen the King

Above: A stool used by Tutankhamen as a child. The curved seat would have held a cushion.

Left: A detail from the second gilt coffin shows the king with his regalia: the khspresh headdress and the crook and flail.

Tutankhaten was still only a child when his older brothers died. Most of his life had been spent at Malkata, across the river from Luxor, where his father had a vast estate with a splendid palace, villas for court officials and numerous other buildings. By the age of four he was attending school with the sons of the nobility and the young princes of Egypt's vassal states, who were brought up at court to ensure political harmony. Mornings would be devoted to reading and writing, and later on to

simple calculations in arithmetic. In the afternoons they would wrestle, practise archery or go swimming. Riding was also popular, and the older boys would sometimes hunt on the edge of the desert for hares, antelopes, gazelles and even ostriches.

Amarna was only a few days' journey down the Nile, and Tutankhaten visited his older brother on several occasions. He usually stayed in the palace of Nefertiti, Akhenaten's beautiful first wife, in

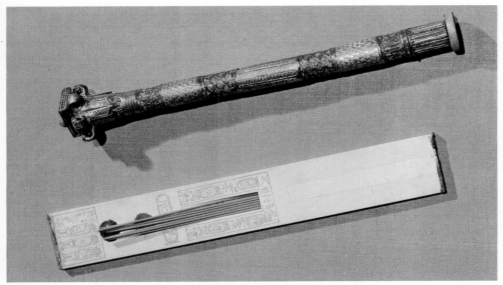

the northern part of the town. Towards the end of his reign, the heretic king lived apart from the queen and took his own daughter, Ankhesenpaaten, as a second wife. She was then about eleven years old, and Akhenaten may have intended her to succeed him, for according to Egyptian custom succession to the throne passed through the female line. Whatever the intention, he had given his daughter a crucial role in the political manoeuvring that would follow his death. When the time came, Nefertiti and the loyal Ay were quick to seize the opportunity. Anxious to maintain the dynasty, they hurriedly married the young queen to her brother-in-law, Tutankhaten.

Events soon showed, however, that while Ay had guaranteed stability in Egypt, the prospect of civil war had only narrowly been averted. The compromise reached with General Horemheb, now a firm ally of the Theban priesthood, involved an almost total abandonment of the Aten cult and a return to strict orthodoxy. When the day of his coronation arrived, after a period of fasting and ritual purification, the nine-year-old boy was escorted to the temple of Amun at Karnak by the highest dignitaries of the court.

Priests masked as gods came to meet him and led him away through

Top left: Tutankhamen's gilt case for writing reeds and his scribe's palette. The colours black and red were made from soot and ochre mixed with gum in the two hollows towards the left of the palette.

Left: An ornamental shield shows Tutankhamen about to kill two lions. The inscription compares his strength to that of the god Montu.

Right: A gilt fly-whisk shows the king (top) hunting ostriches in the desert near Heliopolis and (bottom) returning in triumph to the palace.

a series of halls where the ceremonies were carried out. On his head were placed the white mitre and red cap which combined to form the crown of the two kingdoms. Then he was taken before a shrine of Amun, carved from a single slab of rose granite, and kneeling with his back to the god was 'touched' by the divine presence.

Invested with his new powers, Tutankhaten now returned to take his seat on an ancient throne before the assembled dignitaries. Once again the two crowns were placed upon his head, while masked priests entwined lily and papyrus plants around a pillar to symbolize the unity of North and South. Towards evening, the pharaoh emerged from the temple with all the regalia of traditional kingship, including the famous sceptres of Osiris – the crook of the Southern Kingdom and the flail of the North. The priests of Amun had regained the right to sanctify the transfer of royal authority; symbolically, at least, it was through their mediation that the pharaoh was transformed into an aspect of Horus, the god of the living world.

The name of Akhenaten was no longer mentioned, and the heresy was condemned by all. Nonetheless, Tutankhaten returned with Ay to Amarna and remained there for most of the first four years of his reign. In Thebes, Horemheb assumed the powers of vice-regent and began a vigorous campaign to repair the nation's temples. From Nubia to the Delta, shrines had fallen into desolation; sanctuaries and halls were used as public footpaths. In Tutankhaten's name, he ordered shrines to be rebuilt and priests to be recruited from the nobility of every town. Temples were endowed with both money and precious gifts; slaves were provided as a source of labour. For Karnak itself Horemheb

ordered a statue of Amun in solid gold, inlaid with lapis lazuli and gems.

The next requirement was that the king should return to Thebes. At the same time, his name was officially changed to Tutankhamen, and his wife was to be known as Ankhesenamun. The royal barges

Above: The pharoah's gold-plated throne, decorated with pictures in the Amarnan style.

Left: A detail from the golden throne shows Ankhesenamun anointing the king with oils.

carried their furniture back up the Nile, including even such pieces as the throne, with panels dominated by the globe of Aten extending its bounty to the royal couple with hands of gold. Their main residence may now have been Malkata, but the pharaoh was obliged to make constant journeys to shrines throughout the kingdom, reviving the worship of the gods. Memphis, Medinet el Faiyum, Abydos, were all visited and the pharaoh even renewed a tradition of his ancestors by making sacrifices to the Sphinx at Giza.

The great event of each year, however, held in Thebes during the second month of the Nile floods, was the feast of Opet. For eleven days, it was believed, Amun, his wife Mut and their son Khonsu appeared upon the earth. In honour of this

Above: A carving on the king's ceremonial footstool symbolizes the union of the two kingdoms. On the left, Asian prisoners are bound with the papyrus of the north; on the right, lilies of the south restrain the Africans.

Right: The throne used by Tutankhamen for religious functions. As pharoah he was also high priest of the cult of Amun, the Theban Sun god.

Opposite: Details from the famous painted chest with Tutankhamen vanquishing Egypt's enemies – the Asians (top) and the Africans (bottom).

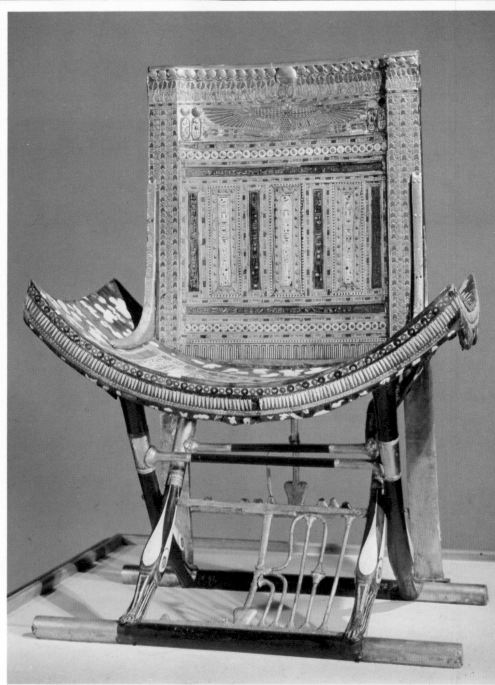

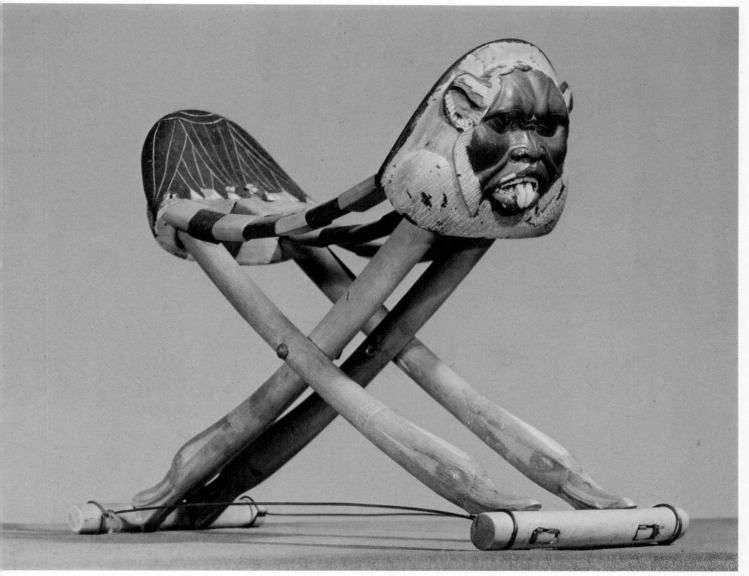

Above: A folding head-rest made of wood and ivory shows two heads of the god Bes, protector against demons. The legs are carved in the form of wild ducks – evil spirits made harmless.

Left: Engravings on the small, gilt shrine show (top) the king pouring perfumed oils into his wife's palm, and (bottom) Tutankhamen shooting wild duck.

'divine emergence' a flotilla of barges and small boats accompanied the statues of the gods in a ceremonial procession along the Nile from Karnak to Luxor.

During the voyage the king would seize an oar, to demonstrate symbolically his responsibility for the journey as the divine high priest of his father's shrine. Throughout the festival, the people feasted and danced and revelled in the narrow streets of Luxor. Eleven days later, after a sacrifice of oxen near the temple, the procession returned to Karnak, this time with Tutankhamen marching along the bank at the head of a military parade.

The costs of these feasts, as well as of all the restoration and endowment of the temples, was borne by the royal exchequer. The very fact that the pharaoh could afford to make such restitution is in itself a powerful testimony to the extraordinary wealth of the Egyptian monarchy. Nonetheless, affairs of state remained pressing and there was an urgent need to strengthen imperial control. In Asia this was done less by military strength — the armies suffered regular defeats during Tutankhamen's reign — than by diplomacy. Horemheb's skill at playing the vassal states off against each other enabled him to keep the empire intact, even though the tribute must have dwindled alarmingly.

A far more vigorous policy was adopted for Nubia. Huy, the son of a

senior official under Amenophis III and a good friend of Tutankhamen, was appointed Viceroy and immediately tightened up the collection of taxes. Nubia's resources were exploited to the full, and Huy's efficiency in organizing public affairs was so welcome after the negligence of the previous reign that even the arts flourished.

Agricultural production was quickly improved and Huy personally supervised the breeding of cattle to enhance the quality of the stock. Miners and wood-cutters were spurred on to greater efforts, while the hunters of the south increased their catch of panthers, elephants and giraffes. Within a very short

40

time Huy sailed back to Thebes with a fleet of barges bearing the tribute of Nubia. Gold, cornelian, jasper, ivory, fine furniture, skins, oxen, slaves and even a giraffe were paraded before the king. With his treasury thus enriched, he could face the future with confidence.

Nonetheless, he had already begun his preparations for death. West of Thebes, where the limestone cliffs rise majestically to the pyramid-shaped mountain of Deir el Bahri, all the pharaohs since Ahmose, the conqueror of Asia, had been laid to rest. At the foot of the cliffs, facing east across the Nile, were the funerary temples where priests performed rituals for years after each pharaoh's

Above: A model boat found in the tomb probably resembles that in which the Viceroy Huy brought tribute from Nubia to Thebes.

Right: A funeral effigy of Tutankhamen wearing the crown of Northern Egypt, with its sacred serpent.

death. The tombs themselves were hidden away in a barren valley beyond the mountain, where they were more likely to escape the attention of robbers. A special village had been built nearby for the workmen, whose main duty in life was to tunnel the royal tombs deep into the rock. Narrow passageways gave access from the surface and their openings were carefully concealed; guards were posted around the valley day and night.

Selection of the two sites was one of the first priorities in the reign of every pharaoh, and Tutankhamen's choice had been made soon after his coronation. Work had probably begun immediately, for it was an immense task to quarry through the limestone with only simple iron tools and muscle-power. Many of the tombs were quite elaborate, consisting of several chambers linked by passageways often extending more than seventy metres into the rock. Construction of the temples was also a major undertaking, for these were the worldly monuments of Egypt's rulers and their scale and ornamentation were a direct reflection of the sovereign's prestige.

When Tutankhamen died suddenly at the age of about 20, neither his tomb nor his temple had been completed. The cause of death remains unknown, but it is generally considered that years of inbreeding had weakened the royal line and that the king had been physically frail from birth. Whatever the truth may be, his early demise left the political compromise between Ay and Horemheb, the strong men of the kingdom, under considerable stress. Little could be done before the burial formalities had been completed – a process lasting some two months – but the contingency planning began at once.

4 Treasures of the Tomb

Left: The solid gold coffin which enclosed the royal mummy.

Below: The jackal god Anubis, who helped Isis repair the body of Osiris, and thus became the god of funerals.

Death for the Ancient Egyptians was not an end to be feared, but rather the threshold to an eternal and presumably pleasurable existence. There were certain obstacles to be confronted, but with careful preparation and strict observance of all the rituals these could normally be overcome. For ordinary people the greatest danger came at the time of judgement, when the jackal god Anubis would weigh their hearts against a feather representing truth. If the scales balanced, the spirits would pass on to their final dwelling place, somewhere in the western desert. Pharaohs, on the other hand, would undergo a spiritual transformation during the long night of the dead, to awake as gods and take their place in the celestial boat which carried the sun god on his daily voyage.

Although it was well-known that the earthly body would never be revived, the Egyptians believed that its preservation was essential and that no-one should be allowed to disturb its rest. Common people were buried in shallow earthen pits, and chemicals in the soil prevented decomposition. For the nobility and pharaohs, however, who were buried in stone tombs, some form of embalming was essential. By the time of Tutankhamen this art had been highly developed and the preparation of a royal corpse for burial required a period of seventy days. The process was associated with the story of Isis, who had collected the pieces of Osiris' body and restored him to eternal life with the aid of Anubis.

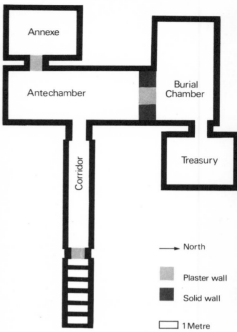

Above: Diagram showing the layout of the tomb, with the rooms as they were named by Howard Carter.

The act of embalming and of mummification was therefore attended with lengthy and elaborate rituals performed by specialist priests.

Reflecting this positive attitude to death, the embalming rooms were known as 'the house of vigour' and black, the colour of funerals, was associated with rebirth, not grief. While the court mourned and men close to the dead pharaoh stopped shaving, as a mark of respect, the workshops of the goldsmiths and cabinet-makers became hives of activity. A wide range of equipment was needed for the burial, and little was ready. In the royal necropolis, the superintendent Maya ordered the labourers to abandon the tomb they had already started and to concentrate instead on a far smaller site which was being prepared for Ay,

Left: One of the tiny gold coffins containing the king's organs. The face may be that of Smenkhkare, Tutankhamen's brother, for whom the coffins were originally intended.

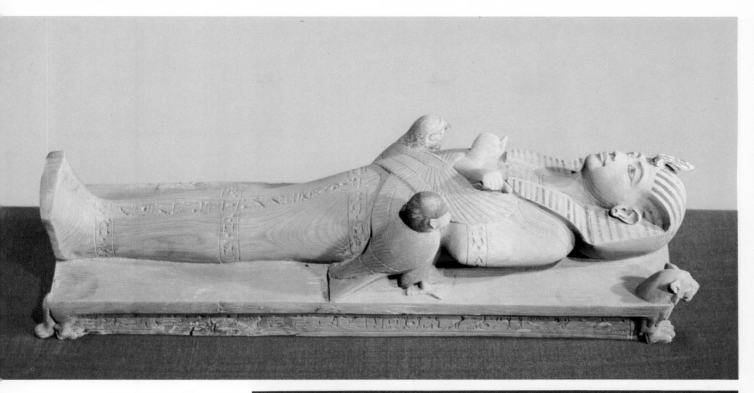

the pharaoh's chief adviser.

As the day of the funeral approached, the finishing touches were hurriedly applied. The brain and viscera had been removed from the royal body, which had then been plunged into a bath of dry natron to absorb all humidity. Only the heart, believed to be the seat of intelligence, was left inside the corpse; the abdomen was filled with aromatic herbs and sealed with a golden plate. As the body was bandaged, using hundreds of yards of fine linen, numerous precious objects were placed between the folds. Necklaces, rings, bracelets, diadems, pendants and amulets were all set carefully in place, each with its own ritual significance.

Once in the tomb, the mummy would be placed in its coffin and drenched with preserving fluids known as unguents. The liver and other internal organs were wrapped separately and put into four tiny coffins and then into jars of unguents. Since time was so short, containers originally intended for Smenkhkare, Tutankhamen's brother, were quickly adapted; they

would be buried with the king in a canopic shrine.

When everything was ready, the mummy, adorned with a magnificent golden mask, was taken to the palace and laid in state on a large animal-shaped couch. Finally, one April morning in 1343 B C, the court broke up from its long period of mourning; the men shaved and the women dressed in simple white linen

Above: Diagram showing the burial chamber with its nest of shrines and mummiform coffins.

Top: A carving of the king's mummy protected by two souls the Ka and the human-headed Ba.

45

tunics. The procession to the tomb was led by 'the Nine Friends of the King', who drew the sledge-like hearse, while priests sprinkled it with sacred milk. Behind them came the courtiers, carrying the burial furniture – thrones, beds, chariots, statuettes, coffers full of jewels, vases and jars containing unguents. In the centre of the procession came a smaller hearse with the canopic urns and bringing up the rear was a large group of women loudly lamenting the passing of the king.

The first part of the journey ended at the funerary temple, where the body would rest a further four days. During a long ceremony a bull was sacrificed and its heart and forefoot presented to the mummy. Ay, officiating in the absence of a son, then took an adze and touched the mouth and eyes of the funerary mask to open the senses to eternal life.

At daybreak the next morning the procession set out for the tomb, which was only just ready. Paintings on the three walls of the burial chamber were still wet, and the fourth wall could not be built until the coffin had been placed inside the massive shrine. During the course of the day, however, everything was installed in its rightful place in the four rooms of the tomb. With the entrance finally sealed, the guests sat down to a funeral banquet prepared in a large tent pitched nearby.

Three thousand years later, when the archaeologists entered the tomb, many of its contents had been moved from their original positions. Enough

Top left: An elegant ivory chest, made for carrying rings during the funeral procession.

Left: The alabaster shrine which held the four canopic urns containing the king's mummified organs. Each corner is protected by a goddess.

Right: The stopper from one of the canopic urns.

evidence remained, however, for them to be fairly certain of the arrangement. The room containing the tomb itself had been plastered up at the last moment, leaving only a narrow space around the large gilt shrine. This in turn was found to contain three more shrines, one within the other, which were designed symbolically to restore to Tutankhamen all the royal prerogatives he had enjoyed on earth.

While the innermost shrine was made in the style of the palaces of the Northern Kingdom, the next two echoed that of the Southern palaces. The largest shrine of all was in the image of a jubilee pavilion, at which kings reigning for thirty years would have their youthful powers renewed by undergoing a ritualized 'death' and rebirth. By the open doors of this last shrine stood a silver trumpet, perhaps to announce the resurrection of the pharaoh, and the effigy of a goose, a symbol of the sun's victory over the shadows.

Within this nest of gilded shrines was a red sandstone sarcophagus containing three coffins, also one inside the other. Here again was evidence of the hasty preparations: to fit the mummy-shaped coffins into the sarcophagus, carpenters had been forced to plane down the feet. Worse still, the granite lid of the sarcophagus had been dropped and broken in two – hurriedly fixed, it was put in place and the crack painted over.

Left: The head of a funerary couch in the form of a cheetah with tears falling from his eyes.

Top right: Head of the cow goddess Hathor, whose body symbolized the vault of heaven. Between her horns she holds an image of the sun.

Right: A senet *board, on which the reborn king would play a game of Hazard.*

The three central coffins, each portraying the pharaoh with a slightly different expression, were of impeccable workmanship. The innermost was of solid gold, the others of gilded wood; and all three were inlaid with precious stones and lapis lazuli. So accurately were they constructed that there was scarcely room to squeeze a little finger into the gap between each coffin.

The Egyptians believed that each person had two souls – the *ka*, a double that would pass on into the next world, and the *ba*, which would continue to hover around the body. The preparations in the tomb were designed to help the *ka*, which would draw on the forces contained in the funerary equipment to make a symbolic journey during the night. On the wall of the burial chamber was a painting of twelve dog-headed baboons and the boat of the sun; after sinking beneath the western

horizon, the sun was thought to travel through the underworld, and if the king's *ka* could complete its transformation, it would enter this boat and rise in splendour with the sun.

In the treasury beside the burial room, therefore, stood the little canopic shrine, so that the vital organs could be reunited with the body. Each corner of the shrine was guarded by a tiny golden goddess. In another chest, two mummified foetuses represented the souls of the king just before rebirth; nearby, a statue of Anubis kept watch for evil spirits. During the course of its journey through the night, the *ka* would have to overcome dangers faced by Osiris long before, and a large amount of equipment was placed in the treasury to make this possible.

Light hunting chariots and weapons stacked against the wall were provided for the god Shed, who

Top left: One of two life-size statues of the king, representing his souls, which guarded the entrance to the burial chamber.

Top right: An ushabti *of Tutankhamen on a papyrus raft, ready to harpoon the demons of the swamp.*

Right: A chest lid showing Ankhesenamun offering mandrakes – a symbol of sexuality – to Tutankhamen.

50

could use them to massacre demons should they dare to attack while the *ka* was still vulnerable. Other effigies would be useful as the soul grew stronger. Known as *ushabtis*, these images of the king were projections of different aspects of his personality, allowing him to deal with any emergency. A statue of Tutankhamen standing in a papyrus boat, ready to throw his harpoon, may refer to Osiris' adventures in the swamps of the Delta, where he was attacked by demons. He saved himself with his harpoon and was later carried to safety on the back of a cheetah.

Of the two other rooms in the royal tomb, the largest was the antechamber, which the archaeologists reached first. This was separated from the burial chamber by the plaster wall. Here were found objects directly affirming the powers of the pharaoh and presumably intended to recreate them during his transformation. As well as two sumptuous thrones, there was an elegant chest with scenes of the king victorious over the Asians and Africans; two gilt chariots, decorated with images of defeated enemies; a bow, parade sticks, jewel boxes and fine linen.

Many of these articles appear to have been used by Tutankhamen while alive, but others were probably made especially for burial. The magnificent golden couches which so impressed Carter as he first peered into the darkness may have been used by the embalmers during the mortuary preparations. Each was in the form of a protective animal deity: the hippopotamus, the cheetah and the cow. Finally, standing guard by the plaster wall were two life-size statues of the king bearing his crook and flail; they represented the *ba* and *ka*.

The last room opened by the archaeologists was to the west of the antechamber with its door facing east, the direction of the dawn. Known as the annexe, this was the chamber of rebirth, where the emphasis was on the pleasures of life. Here, as Osiris, the king would once again make love to his faithful wife, so that the new pharaoh, the Horus, could be conceived. Food and drink was provided for the love-feast – wildfowl and beef and the finest wines.

A small gilt shrine found near the door of the annexe may have contained statuettes of the king and queen; these were probably stolen by the robbers. On the side panels the royal couple are shown in attitudes of great tenderness. There, and on the ivory lid of a chest shaped like a desk, Ankhesenamun offers her husband bunches of lotus and

papyrus mingled with mandrakes – a symbol of sexuality.

Elsewhere in the chamber were reminders of childhood: toys and playthings like a sling, a set of castanets and a small firelighter. It was a room of dalliance and leisure; yet even here was a grim reminder of the dangers Tutankhamen faced in his journey through the night. On a large, thirty-squared board he would play a game of chance named *senet*, relying on fortune and divine protection to lead him through the traps and obstacles laid by demons. At the end, however, victory was assured. The preparations had been

made with meticulous care; nothing had been forgotten. In the passage leading from the tomb the priests had placed a final, sacred image: a head of the reborn king, like his father Re, rising in a lotus flower from the primeval ocean.

Above: The small gilt shrine which originally contained statuettes of Tutankhamen and Ankhesenamun.

Left: Details from the gilt shrine. (top) The queen brings flowers and perfumed oils to the king. (bottom) The queen fastens a pendant round the king's neck.

53

5 Horemheb's Revenge

Tutankhamen's death had thrown Egypt into political confusion. The retreat from religious heresy had been too rapid for any lasting stability to be achieved. The king's councillor, Ay, had also been Akhenaten's first minister and was viewed with great suspicion by Horemheb, still in control of the imperial armies. With no son or close male relative to marry, the widow Ankhesenamun was in a fearfully vulnerable position. Only she could confer legitimacy on a new pharaoh, yet there was no-one in or near the royal family who would conceivably be acceptable to the priesthood and the army. Within seventy days, the all too brief interlude between death and burial, she would have to make her choice.

By a strange quirk of history we know exactly what happened next, for a Hittite prince, writing only a generation later, recounts the story. 'The widowed queen of Egypt sent an ambassador to my father and wrote to him in these terms: "My husband is dead and I have no son. People say that you have many sons. . . . Give me one of your sons and he will be my husband and lord of the land of Egypt." Because my father was generous, he granted the lady's request and decided to send his son.'

Perhaps Ankhesenamun made this proposal on Ay's advice. The Hittites had recently risen to power north of Syria and were beginning

Right: A mirror case in the shape of an ankh, *the symbol of life, inlaid with the hieroglyph for Nebkheprure, Tutankhamen's coronation name.*

Left: The head of Tutankhamen rising from the primeval ocean in a lotus blossom – symbol of the King's resurrection as a god.

to pose a serious threat to the empire; a diplomatic marriage might prevent hostilities. Nonetheless, this was a desperate measure and highly dangerous. The queen was rejecting every Egyptian suitor in favour of a foreigner, a potential enemy. When Prince Zannaza of the Hittites attempted the long journey south, he was intercepted by Horemheb's guards and put to death. This in turn provoked an attack on Syria by the Hittite armies, but the imperial defences were strong enough to withstand the crisis. Ankhesenamun, however, had no more room for manoeuvre and a decision had to be made. On the morning of the seventieth day she announced the appointment of Ay as co-regent.

Now in his sixties, an old man by Egyptian standards, Ay performed the ceremony of 'the opening of the mouth and eyes' which was traditionally done by the heir to the throne. It seems likely that only his age persuaded Horemheb to tolerate this development, for the army leader must have had hopes of becoming pharaoh himself. In any event, Ay could not hope to survive much longer. Immediately after the burial, he ordered work to begin on his own funerary temple, and the large tomb originally intended for Tutankhamen was also completed.

In this climate of uncertainty, even the most menial employees of the crown sought to protect themselves against the future. For the guards and workmen of the royal necropolis, this could only mean plundering graves, and the treasures of Tutankhamen's funeral still gleamed in the mind's eye. On at least two occasions, a bold and determined gang tunnelled their way in through the doors and passageways. Their main targets were jewels and the rich unguents used in preserving the body: these could easily be sold and were extremely valuable. The

thieves even took wineskins to carry away the precious liquids – the remains of one were discovered in the tomb.

Before they had removed very much, however, the break-in was reported to Maya, the superintendent, who sent his inspectors to investigate. The robbers were very nearly caught red-handed and one

Left : A detail of the small gilt shrine shows Ankhesenamun in a garden. Behind her Tutankhamen shoots wild ducks, which the Egyptians regarded as evil spirits.

Below : An ushabti *of Tutankhamen wearing the red crown of Northern Egypt.*

of them dropped a bundle of gold rings as he fled for safety. The inspectors found the rooms in disarray, but decided against a formal re-arrangement. Instead they tidied up almost at random, stuffing the empty chests full of jewels, material and anything else that would fit. The door was hastily resealed with the official sign of the necropolis, and Maya ordered the entrance to be blocked with a layer of heavy rubble.

Within four years of his accession Ay was dead. Ankhesenamun seems also to have died during this period, for nothing more is known of her. The crisis of the royal family had finally arrived, and the crown was seized by Horemheb, aided by the priests of Amun. Legitimacy was achieved by his marrying Mutnedjmet, the sister of Nefertiti, but the new pharaoh showed nothing but hatred for his predecessors.

All the monuments dedicated to the gods by Tutankhamen were taken over: the dead king's name was hammered out of the magnificent colonnade at Luxor and replaced by that of Horemheb. Akhenaten's capital at Amarna was almost entirely demolished. More ominous still, the names of Akhenaten, Tutankhamen and Ay were erased from the court records, which now declared Horemheb the direct successor to Amenophis III.

An era of violent reform was announced by the 'Edict of Horemheb', a lengthy decree engraved on a slab of stone which was erected at Karnak. Describing the lamentable state of the country, the pharaoh declared his intention to restore order at any cost. He was determined to protect the poor from the abuses of the government and the army; corrupt officials would be punished by having their noses cut off or being sent into exile. Meanwhile the process of restoring the

Top left: An alabaster ibex, inlaid with the hieroglyph for Nebkheprure, Tutankhamen's coronation name.

Top right: The princess Mutnedjmet, wife of Horemheb, shown sitting at the prow of an alabaster boat in the form of an ibex.

Right: An alabaster jar showing a hunting scene. The lion on the lid bears the name of Tutankhamen.

priesthood to its former powers was accelerated, with the cult of Amun the main beneficiary. Buildings dedicated to Aten were demolished to provide materials for three monumental gateways at Amun's temple and a magnificent avenue of sphinxes was erected between Karnak and Luxor.

Secure in the support of both army and priesthood, Horemheb now turned against his predecessors with a vengeance. Ay's tomb and funerary temple were ransacked and abandoned. Even the graves of courtiers were desecrated – the burial chapel of Huy, once the viceroy in Nubia, was attacked and pictures of Tutankhamen were obliterated from its walls. Throughout the kingdom the names of Ay and Tutankhamen were hammered off monuments and the sanctuaries of Aten were destroyed. The dead pharaohs had been consigned to oblivion – deprived of the rites and prayers which should nourish their souls, and wiped out of the historical record.

Thus Tutankhamen, a king whose short life had been spent in atonement for mistakes committed by his elders, was pursued beyond the grave. Yet even the remorseless Horemheb could not expunge his name completely. Beneath the plaster of a memorial at Karnak, the mason had cut the hieroglyph deep into the stone, where it remained concealed. Moreover, by leaving his tomb intact, Horemheb unwittingly secured the young king's destiny: within days of the discovery a full 3000 years later, Tutankhamen had become the most famous of all the Egyptian pharaohs.

Left: The back of a cedar chair decorated with Tutankhamen's name. The central figure is the spirit of years without number.

Glossary

AHMOSE: Pharaoh who successfully drove the Hyksos out of Egypt, inaugurating an era of imperial expansion known as the New Kingdom.

AKHENATEN: Name adopted by Amenophis IV, brother of Tutankhamen, in honour of the god Aten, whom he worshipped exclusively.

AKHETATEN: 'The Horizon of the Globe'. Royal city founded by Akhenaten at Amarna.

AMARNA: Site of Akhenaten's royal city, Akhetaten.

AMENOPHIS III: Father of Tutankhamen, with his main palace at Malkata, for several years co-regent with Akhenaten.

AMENOPHIS IV: Brother of Tutankhamen who changed his name to Akhenaten.

AMUN: Sun god of Thebes who, identified with Re, became the supreme god of Egypt during the Middle and New Kingdoms.

ANKHESENPAATEN: Daughter of Nefertiti and Akhenaten, who married her father towards the end of his life and later became the bride of Tutankhamen. Her name was subsequently changed to Ankhesenamun.

ANUBIS: Jackal god associated with the afterlife. He helped Isis to restore Osiris to eternal life.

ATEN: The supreme god Re in his material aspect as the sun's globe. Worshipped by Akhenaten as the sole provider of life.

AY: Senior minister under Akhenaten and Tutenkhamen, whom he succeeded as pharaoh. Possibly the father of Nefertiti.

HOREMHEB: General in charge of the imperial armies under Akhenaten, Tutankhamen and Ay, whom he succeeded as pharaoh. Leader of reaction against the Amarnan heresy.

HORUS: Son of Isis and Osiris, who avenged his father's murder by killing Seth. 'The eye of Horus', lost in this struggle, is a symbol of the sun; Horus himself is identified with the rising sun and with the pharaoh during his life on earth. He is often shown with the head of a falcon.

ISIS: Wife of Osiris, who collected the scattered pieces of his body and restored him to eternal life with the aid of Anubis.

MAYA: Superintendent of the royal necropolis in Thebes.

MUTNEDJMET: Sister of Nefertiti who probably married Horemheb, thus conferring legitimacy on his succession to the throne.

NEBKHEPRURE: Coronation name of Tutankhamen.

NECROPOLIS: 'City of the dead', or cemetery.

NEFERTITI: First wife of Akhenaten, by whom she had at least six daughters.

NEPHTHYS: Goddess, sister of Isis.

NUBIA: Area on the borders of modern Egypt and Sudan. Conquered by Ancient Egyptians during the Middle Kingdom.

OSIRIS: Son of Re and husband of Isis, he succeeded his father as king of the universe but was murdered by his brother Seth. Restored to life by Isis and Anubis, he became lord of the afterlife.

RE: The sun god, creator of the universe. Originally associated with the pharaohs of Memphis; later adopted and 'amalgamated' with Amun by the Theban priesthood.

SARCOPHAGUS: Heavy stone coffin.

SCARAB: Beetle regarded by Egyptians as a symbol of immortality.

SMENKHKARE: Brother of Akhenaten and Tutankhamen. Briefly co-regent with Akhenaten.

TUTANKHATEN: Birth name of Tutankhamen.

UNGUENTS: Precious oils used for preserving corpses.

USHABTI: Royal funeral statue designed to assist pharaoh in his mystical transformation into a god.